TINKER

ANDREW ALDRED

chipmunkapublishing
the mental health publisher

All rights reserved, no part of this publication may be reproduced by any means, electronic, mechanical photocopying, documentary, film or in any other format without prior written permission of the publisher.

Published by
Chipmunkapublishing
United Kingdom

http://www.chipmunkapublishing.com

Copyright © ANDREW ALDRED 2024

ISBN   978-1-78382-6827

TINKER

This Book is dedicated to My Darling Jane
and Monty the cat

ANDREW ALDRED

Pissed Off

I have had tonsilitis recently.
And I feel like I have been slapped senseless.
I have a headache, a sore throat and a sore head.
I have let down my defences.
I thought they were off my back.
But this illness just carries on and on
People are pissed off with me.
And I am pissed off with them.
They want to ask the impossible
And they have done all along.
I am a disabled man who is getting older.
And they will not let me sleep.
They keep me wide awake and worried.
I have had this illness for forty years.
I wish they would all move on
Get a life of their own and leave me alone.
I have absolutely nothing to offer them.
Why the hell do they want to bother with me?
I am thoroughly pissed off and I hope they are happy.

ANDREW ALDRED

I Could Have Been Gay

Anybody could be gay, and a lot are.
But their way of life and their culture
Has never been something that appealed to me.
You can go on about loving your fellow man.
But there is nothing in it for me.
Except pain and an endless illness
Anybody can always change their sexuality.
Start all over again at any age.
But I suppose you realise that is not for me.
There is more to my life than sex.
And I suppose we can all be bitter.
The sea might turn white one day.
Or the sun might stop shining.
I could have been gay if I wanted.
There is a hell of a lot of things in this life.
That do not suit me and never will.

TINKER

Poorer

We are all going to be poorer now.
Whether we are wealthy or not
We are all going to have less.
Do teachers and nurses not see the news?
Do the rail workers think they are worth more?
We are all going to have to get on with it.
Accept less money and make ends meet.
No more foreign holidays for a lot of people
If you can eat and heat, you are lucky.
Sell your car and catch the bus.
Or buy a bicycle and pedal around on that.
While you try to find money for your mortgage
And your wife and children's food and clothing
Everybody is feeling the pinch and angry.
We blame the government, but we create the wealth.
And everybody wants to put themselves first.
We all have a value and get what we are worth.
You can fight on with your strikes.
But you know you are going to be disappointed.
Most of us are little people on not much money.
We all must swallow our pride and do something.
The government will do its best to keep us afloat.
If you can afford to strike you probable get too much money

ANDREW ALDRED

Not the Same

There are a lot of people and a lot of walks of life.
I am a citizen of Bolton even if I am an outcast.
I really would not want to be anybody else.
They pay me because I am disabled.
Not for any other stupid reasons you might suppose.
I am out of tune with a lot of people.
But I do what I must and obey the law.
In a lot of ways, I am no different to you.
I have a house, a car and a girlfriend.
I also have some sort of family around me.
And I have enough to occupy most of my time.
I could not live and die for the army.
They wanted more than I could give them.
And I cannot live and die for the rest of you.
Because I am a stubborn bastard and I do not want to
But I live in your town and maybe in your street.
You have seen me anywhere and everywhere.
This is one town, but we are all different

TINKER

Ruin it for Everyone.

I am so tired of these people who are so small minded.
They want to ruin everything and cause maximum disruption.
You cannot watch the football or go to the coronation.
Without some set of twerps wanting to ruin it for you
And put across their pathetic point of view on what should be a good day.
Let King Charles and his followers have their coronation.
Let them watch their teams while they play football.
Hold us all to ransom and you will do yourselves no good
You will not change the way of the world so why bother?
Give the people what they want, and you will get your reward.
Ruin it for everyone and you will end up being vilified.
And instead of being noticed you will be ignored.

ANDREW ALDRED

Covering it with Grass

I got my pickaxe out and dug the flowerbed up.
It took an hour and a half of hard work.
I removed all the bulbs that were left loose.
And replaced the soil that I had removed.
Covering it with grass seed and more soil
The flower bed had always looked a mess most of the year.
And grass is a cheap replacement when it adjoins a lawn.
Within a month the grass had grown, and it looked better.
Covering it with grass has given my garden a cheap makeover.

TINKER

Light Switches

I had been phased by the light switch the last time I looked.
But I was determined to replace it with a new one.
To go with the plug sockets, I had put in last year.
I drew a diagram of the wires and where they fitted.
And I got the right sort of switch to replace the old one.
I switched off the mains and secured all the connections.
And within twenty minutes I had a new, working light switch.

Painting Again

I wanted to get a new carpet in my bedroom.
So, I cut the old one up and removed it.
And set about painting my room with some white paint.
Gradually the room became white once again.
And then I did the gloss work with some ancient paint
That had been in her mother's garage for twenty years.
It dried slightly off-white, but it will do.
Then I got my room professionally carpeted
And put everything back in the same place as before.
Then I started in the kitchen which I had touched up
But the colour was wrong, and it needed doing again.
I had a couple of spare cans of paint the same colour.
And there was plenty to do the job and some left over.
For a couple of days effort my kitchen is the same shade of red
And I can down my brushes and put my decorating sheets away.

TINKER

Boarding Up a Window

They had broken into the garage at her mother's house.
Which we had to leave vacant while the old lady was in care
The window at the back of the garage needed boarding up.
So, I went to B and Q and got some cheap timber.
With a tongue on one side and a groove on the other
I cut the timber to length to make an oblong shape.
Fixing it together with two stays at top and bottom
Then I screwed it into place using the old window frame
If they want to break in again, it will take a good half hour.
The window is boarded up and the garage is secure again.

ANDREW ALDRED

Re-housing the Cat

Her daughter had two cats and a dog.
But one of the cats was unhappy with his lot.
He was the first pet she took care of
And the other cat and dog came afterwards.
Perhaps unsurprisingly he feels pushed out.
The other cat and the dog get on well.
He was not able to participate and felt left out.
We have been thinking about getting a pet.
And so, Jane's daughter has a solution.
We got a litter tray and some cat litter.
We made the house cat-proof and got a scratching post.
And we collected out new family member today.
He seems to be settling in with Jane well.
She has the furry friend she wanted.
And I will be glad to say hello to Monty every day.
The cat has been re-housed and is settling in.

TINKER

Cleaning Up My Act

I spend too much money on my record collection.
And if I am going to finance my next book
I am going to have to stop buying records for a few months.
Being a wild-eyed gambler has never appealed to me.
And those gambling firms are making money for themselves.
And the people who use them will only end up poor.
I take prescription drugs, but I do not take illegal ones.
And the four cans of lager I used to have at night are gone.
I try to follow a healthy diet and get regular exercise.
I am careful how I drive my car and need to make it last.
I must make my money last and try to save some.
I will be cleaning up my act until I drop dead.

ANDREW ALDRED

Mending the Gutter

The gutter had a small gap between the bottom of it and the drain.
So, I bought a connecting sleeve to fit over the gap.
I cut it to length and sawed a quarter segment out of it.
It was just the right size to clip over the existing gutter.
And join to the waste pipe in the ground underneath.
I fitted it and clipped the remaining segment in at the back.
And now the gutter goes down to the ground in one piece.

TINKER

Fixing the Kitchen

I bought some runners for the drawers on the internet.
Took the broken ones off and made them right.
I glued the drawer fronts back on to the drawers.
And I rebuilt the rotten skirting boards with filler.
I cleaned the grease off the top of the cupboards.
And I cleaned the oven with oven cleaner.
I cleaned behind the cooker and the washing machine.
There is always something to do in the kitchen as well as cook.
Lately I seem to spend a lot of time fixing the kitchen.

ANDREW ALDRED

Keys

They seem to pick on people who are single and isolated.
They will steal your spare keys while you are unaware.
Some of the people you trust really do not care.
If you are living alone, you had better beware.
If they cannot have your belongings, they want your body.
They will do anything to make you feel their pain.
Please realise you get what is yours for yourself.
If you are ill, you do not need to bow down to the community.
They can get on by themselves without you and me.
Guard your keys and look after them carefully.
If there are ghosts in your house, they probably have keys.
You can always change your locks if you are concerned about security.

TINKER

Record Collection

Some of it I bought brand new, but it is mostly second hand.
I bought outer sleeves for everything and spare inner sleeves.
I glued together the sleeves that had come apart.
I replaced old records with more modern re-releases.
And bought better copies of old favourites over the years.
I sold or got rid of things that were unacceptable to me.
And I gradually got what I wanted and shed the rest.
I bought replacement cases for my cd's and scratch remover.
I cleaned my vinyl with washing up liquid and water.
And I have transformed what was second hand cast offs.
Into something that I like and can now be proud of
I bought some cd stands the same and all second hand.
And metal cases for my vinyl which I keep in racks.
Everything is clean, tidy and ordered with my favourite tracks.

Brothers

Kevin Sinfield and Rob Burrows are national news.
They are all I have seen on the TV for months.
And I am more aware of motor neurone disease than ever.
Rugby is a hard sport, and this can be the result.
You can be a rugby player or have any other choice of career.
Just do not think you will never get hurt and you will live forever.
You will have to die of something whatever it is.
And it will invariably be difficult however long it takes.
I am glad for Sinfield and Burrows and what they have done.
But it is time for something else to be shown on the news.
They are rugby players and brothers and I wish I was more like them.

TINKER

Graffiti

The kids broke her mother's garage window and put graffiti on the door.
I am glad to say their father has made the wall taller.
By putting some extra concrete blocks between the fence posts
And hopefully encouraging the little buggers to stay in their own garden.
We got in touch with the police, but nothing will get done.
And I have cleared the graffiti off the door and the back window.
With brasso and a scouring pad and a lot of effort
It looks alright again, and I hope it will be left alone.
And maybe the kids can find something better to occupy themselves.

ANDREW ALDRED

Paying More for Green Energy

They called me on the telephone today.
Talking about roof panels and heat pumps
Saying they had government grants for thousands.
But they still want more than I can afford.
I cannot pay ten thousand pounds for roof panels.
I already have a gas boiler that works well.
If they want me to have a heat pump it had better be worth it
They said they would give me a free quote.
But they do not seem to be getting back to me on that.
So, I will have to see how long my boiler lasts.
And hope things have come down in price by then.
It will be enough of a headache getting an electric car.
And you know I will not be able to afford a new one.
Go green and pay through the nose for it!
I guess I will be stuck with old technology for now.

TINKER

Hot Potato

They dropped him like a hot potato.
He has been on prime-time TV for thirty years.
He declared himself homosexual and had an affair.
And he has a brother who committed sex crimes.
Is he the most unfortunate man on the planet?
Or is there more to this story than we know?
Well, they seem to want to tear him to pieces.
His talent agency no longer wants to know him.
Luckily for him he has made a lot of money.
And can probably afford to never work again.
I just hope he is not the next Rolf Harris
Or another Jimmy Savile who has remained unknown.
But he has become invisible almost overnight.
Philip Schofield is a man with a lot of secrets.

ANDREW ALDRED

Foot Pump

I bought a new foot pump for my tyres today.
It is the best purchase I have made recently.
Seven pounds ninety-nine and it works like a dream.
It even has a pressure gauge built in
The old pump was worn and buckled.
And is now only fit for the bin.
You can buy a lot of fancy gear for your tyres.
But you cannot beat an old-fashioned foot pump.

TINKER

Fixing my Car

I fix my car myself.
Apart from when it needs servicing.
And when it needs to pass its MOT
I scraped the front spoiler on some concrete.
So, I filled it with fibreglass and painted it.
I have vacuumed the inside of it.
I washed it recently and pumped up the tyres.
I have oil, coolant and screen wash inside it.
And I will somehow get another five years.
Out of this car before I scrap it.
Until then I will be happy to be fixing my car

ANDREW ALDRED

Clearing a House

They have finally got permission to sell the house.
I have been busy looking after the garden.
But we can now start to clear the house.
We have emptied all the furniture.
And arranged with local charities to take it away.
Jane and her sister will sift through all their mothers' belongings.
Which we have put in boxes downstairs
What is left will go to charity or be disposed of
Then the house will be ready to sell, and we can relax.

TINKER

Jack of All Trades

In my life as a disabled man, I dabble with a lot of things.
From installing plug sockets and light switches to mending cars
Landscaping my garden and painting fences and rooms in my house
If there is anything I can turn my hand to I will get it done
I might not be in the best of health, but I am not lazy.
As a soldier I was a jack of all trades and master of none
And I am the same now I am in civilian life.
I carry on the best way I can and hope the money will take care of itself.

ANDREW ALDRED

Leaving a Mess

The Russians have just blown up a huge dam in Ukraine.
It is in territory they are occupying now.
Could they at last be planning some sort of withdrawal?
They like to create havoc wherever they go.
And leave a large mess for the Ukrainians to clear up.
There is a lot of bad feeling in the war between Russia and Ukraine
The Russians thought the Ukrainians would be subservient.
That they would be able to march in and liberate a country.
They are getting used to the fact that they are not welcome.
Russia is getting a taste of its own medicine with Ukrainian drone strikes.
The war has dragged on for long enough and I hope it will end.
Ukraine has earned the right to join NATO and be protected.
Putin must face the music with his own people and take responsibility.
It has been a bitter war and the country has been left in a mess.

TINKER

Fighting the Press

Everybody knows Prince Harry is right in what he says.
But the people he is taking to court have covered their tracks.
There are no traces of anything and there is no evidence.
As somebody who has a paranoid illness, I can tell Harry.
That he should be grateful for the life he has got.
And that even a Prince cannot change the way of the world
He needs to move on from his first girlfriend because he is married.
He has plenty of money and he should not be spending it on this.
I know it has been terribly hard on his mother and himself.
But he needs to step back and let it be for his own sanity.

ANDREW ALDRED

Key Fob

There was an electrical storm in Farnworth last night.
I came in from a day's work and washed my clothes.
But I had left my car keys in my pocket when I did.
And when I came to start my car later it would not work
I called out the RAC to get my car fixed through my insurance.
But they took hours and I tried to start the car again.
This time it started up, but the key fob was still faulty.
I took it apart and left it to dry out the next night.
And I got a new key fob for my car from Amazon.
And I will assemble it using the parts from the old one.
A brand-new key fob would cost a lot of money.
But a key fob from Amazon and a bit of effort will cost fifteen quid.

Stupid Protesters

These protesters just do not understand the situation.
They are attacking the problem from the wrong angle.
They should be actively involved in halting climate change.
They need to be working to save the planet instead of causing disruption.
They can save water and recycle things in their own households.
They can eliminate their own use of fossil fuels.
They can get jobs in the renewable energy industry.
They do not need to spread orange powder everywhere.
They do not need to ruin expensive artwork.
Everybody is concerned about climate change as it is.
But you are not going to save the planet by ruining a flower show.
Stupid protesters just get everyone's backs up and create chaos.

ANDREW ALDRED

Getting my Money Back

I wanted a manual for something from the internet.
So, I ordered it and waited for it to come by email.
But nothing came so I complained and asked for a refund.
But there was no response, so I telephoned my bank.
And gave the details of the transaction to recover the money.
They have at least got back to me with details of a refund.
And I will get my money back off them if it is at all possible

Criminals or Politicians?

Nicola Sturgeon has been arrested recently along with her husband.
No wonder the SNP is doing less well in the polls.
When the leaders want to take the party's money for themselves
Donald Trump spends his life evading going to prison.
And trying to slow down the legal system while he runs for president.
And Boris Johnson is still protesting his innocence over partygate
While people try to discipline him and stop him being a politician
Vladimir Putin wants to carry on smashing Ukraine to pieces.
And somehow thinks he is entirely right in doing so.
There is civil war in Sudan because two men cannot agree.
The people running the place are more misguided than the rest of us.
We must put our faith in criminals because nobody else wants the job.

ANDREW ALDRED

Too Hot

Recently there has been a heatwave and I cannot get anything done.
For the simple reason that it is too hot to do anything
Even if I do a simple task in this weather, I end up in a pool of sweat.
Everyone on the road seems to be suffering from road rage.
And everywhere you look everyone's tempers are frayed.
If I want to work in the garden, I will have to wait for cooler weather.
As an older man with asthma, I cannot cope with the way things are.
The heat is overpowering now, and I hope it changes soon.

Demise of a Dictator

Russia's Wagner forces recently marched on Moscow.
And then their leader went away to Belarus.
To live a quiet life and never be seen again
Putin must be living in fear at this moment in time.
Of a knock on the door when he is taken away
Or of a mob seizing him and hanging him in public
Russia really needs a dose of perestroika right now.
And Ukraine and the rest of the world need an end to the war.
We could all do with someone more moderate in charge of Russia
Putin was wrong to go to war with Ukraine in every way.
It was an example of a power crazed dictator going too far.
It is clear he needs to be removed and replaced.
The demise of Vladimir Putin cannot come soon enough.

ANDREW ALDRED

Getting Help

If my partner had been a middle-aged white woman
If she was not disabled and had a decent job
She would have been the first to get treatment.
But as it is we are struggling to get anywhere
A female doctor in her twenties fobbed us off.
The receptionist at the surgery did not want to know.
We had to go to an out of hours surgery at night.
To get diagnosed properly by an African doctor.
And hopefully now things will start to happen.
Disadvantaged people are always last in the queue.
Getting help for Jane will always be difficult.

Helping the Homeless

Prince William has always taken more than a passing interest.
In the homeless population and the problems, they have
And I cannot deny his heart is in the right place.
And his support is worth a lot to the people he is helping.
I know he has three huge royal mansions to live in
But at least he is interested in doing something for the rest of us.
They need to get all these people off the streets.
For the good of everyone, not just themselves
I have been homeless myself and will sometimes give money.
But I get sick of being hassled outside shops and in car parks.
These people need to live in buildings like the rest of us.
And that would make them responsible and integrate them.
If you give the homeless something you will get something back
Helping the homeless always starts with giving them somewhere to live.

Lost at Sea

They should never have let a vehicle that had not been tested.
Go down half a mile to the ocean floor with five people.
Are they really that surprised it imploded?
Some of these adventurers really are bloody crazy.
The result is five dead people, one a billionaire.
And five families who have lost a loved one to the ocean.
A submariner said this should be the end of these expeditions.
When he did the news commentary about this tragic event
When you are lost at sea it is not often the case you are found again

TINKER

Potatoes and Onions

I grow more potatoes and onions every year.
In pots and trays in my back garden
They are easy to plant, and I leave them to grow.
And when it gets to midsummer, I harvest them.
I end up eating potatoes for about a month.
But it saves on my food bill, and they are good.
It has been a tradition with me for a few years.
Potatoes and onions will help ease my cost-of-living fears.

ANDREW ALDRED

No to the Nanny State

Labour wants to give us all jobs looking after each other.
I look after my girlfriend and myself and that is enough.
They want people who are fit for nothing to do something.
The conservatives at least see to it that we get benefits.
And all any government has been able to do for me.
Is give me the money to survive and leave me alone.
Then at least I can have some autonomy and be responsible.
Rather than have some set of left-wing lunatics to answer to
Who want to take all my money for themselves and do nothing?
I do not want a nanny state and I do not want Keir Starmer
The labour party are all a bunch of would-be social workers.
They are no good to me, never have been and never will be.

French Riots

The media wants to stoke people's anger against the police.
I see it happening every day on the news in this country.
But we also must look to the police for help.
And when the youth of a country is tearing it to bits
Burning out cars and buildings and rioting at night
The police very rightly must deal with the problem.
If the French protests were peaceful and they met with government
I am sure they would get a better result than they have got.
They turn everybody against them instead of sorting out the problem.
And when people behave like this you end up sympathising with the police
There have been about a thousand arrests in these French riots.
People have let their feeling be known but they are no further forward.
Change would be there if people wanted it, but they do not.

ANDREW ALDRED

Trying to Bring the Government Down

All these striking workers have one thing in common.
That is that they mostly vote for the labour party.
Another thing they have in common is that they are blind to reality.
You can vote for change, but situations must be created.
If you want to be richer your economy must support that
Nobody wants to admit that Rishi Sunak knows something.
About business and money management and how to create wealth
A vote for the labour party will leave everyone worse off.
Because they have always wasted money on social welfare
There is this idea that the state will look after everything.
But people need to take charge of their own lives.
People seem to want to bring the government down.
But what will replace it will be something worse in the form of labour?

Artificial Intelligence

This is an area of computer programming.
That is becoming dangerously out of control.
They can clone anybody on god's green earth.
And put out false information as if it is from them.
It will get into the wrong hands and has done already.
Impersonating Zelensky, Trump and Martin Lewis
You cannot believe anything you see on TV anymore.
And you should not trust anything on your phone or computer.
If I were you, I would keep out of social media.
If you get too popular you will get scammed
Artificial intelligence has always been insidious.
It can learn how to do everything better than us.
In the wrong hands it could be totally disastrous
Artificial intelligence will rule this world in the future.

ANDREW ALDRED

Silly Socialists

They are full of themselves and their own importance.
Teachers, Doctors, rail workers and the rest of them
They are socialists but all they are after is money.
They are not content with the same wages as the rest of us.
They go against their own principles with their actions.
They think what they are doing is for the good of their professions.
What would be good is if they all left to do something else.
If they were fit to earn millions that is what they would be doing
But they are not, and we all must suffer because of them.
I wish they would all grow up and live in the real world.
Where you do not get everything off your mum and dad
And the government and the state are not responsible.
Silly socialists will bring us all down with their capitalist ideas.

TINKER

Honest Politician

I saw an interview with Angela Rayner today.
It took place in her constituency of Ashton Under Lyne
Everybody knew her and she was engaged in the community.
She is deputy leader of the labour party as well as an MP.
She has good morals and ethics but what about her business sense?
She admitted to having friends in the Conservative party.
And she said her relationship with Keir Starmer was a working one.
She appeared to be an approachable and accountable person.
But is she really hard-headed enough to see this country through?
Difficult decisions have to be made and people prioritised.
Angela Rayner knows what life is like on a level with you and me.
But is that really what is needed to restore this crumbling country?

ANDREW ALDRED

No More Money

The doctors and the rest of them will be disappointed.
You can be a doctor or God, but you will only get so much.
You can vote them out, but will you get more under labour.
You can go on strike for the sake of it if you want.
But that will not get your job done for you.
There are seven and a half million people needing treatment.
And you will have to accept the offer and get on with it.
Or leave the profession, go private or go overseas.

High Profile Targets

There have been a few men of dubious sexuality targeted by the media recently.
These are Huw Edwards, Kevin Spacey and Phillip Schofield
Kevin Spacey has gone to trial but has he broken the law?
Consent can be a very subjective thing if you want to argue about it.
Phillip Schofield and Huw Edwards have disappeared overnight.
Huw Edwards is receiving treatment in a mental hospital.
Are these people being targeted because of their sexuality?
I would say they are and should have been left alone.
The media always wants to bring down high profile targets.
Shooting these people down sells newspapers and television programs.

ANDREW ALDRED

Last of the Old Guard

The golden age of tennis is all but over.
Novak Djokovic lost at Wimbledon today.
Federer and Nadal are all but retired.
Marcos Alcaraz, a twenty-year-old Spaniard
Is the new champion and world number one?
It takes someone special to achieve twenty grand slams.
And the new players will have their work cut out.
Djokovic, Federer and Nadal will be gone soon.
There was Borg, McEnroe and then Sampras.
But the likes of these great players will not be seen again.
Djokovic was the last of the old guard and he fought.
But a younger, fitter man beat him, and he looked his age.

TINKER

Accountable with Money?

Keir Starmer has been on TV recently.
And he said he would be accountable with money.
But historically this is not labour's strong point.
Is he a conservative under the guise of a labour leader?
He cannot support public sector worker's strikes.
He realises there is simply no money to pay them.
And he will have to prioritise the same things as conservatives.
He tries to claim some sort of moral high ground.
Saying you can trust us, but you cannot trust them.
But everybody has run out of ideas and inspiration.
We are all struggling to get by and counting the pennies.

ANDREW ALDRED

Slap on the Wrist

Ukraine wants to join NATO immediately.
But Russia would be extremely annoyed.
And the rest of us feel we have intervened enough.
Without starting the third world war all over again
We have all had a vested interest in Ukraine.
But Ukraine joining NATO is very subjective.
Vladimir Putin has had a slap on the wrist from us.
Ukraine has been decimated and we are so sorry.
But at least it will retain its freedom and nationality.
We want to keep the world intact without change.

Pray for a Miracle

The extreme weather conditions are everywhere.
Sixty thousand died in Europe due to the heat.
There are floods in India and South Korea
Typhoons have swept across America.
And the hottest ever temperature is coming.
The seas are getting warmer and marine life is dying.
I cannot see any way out of this in the near future.
All anybody can do is pray for a miracle and hope God listens.

ANDREW ALDRED

Tinker

Our pet cat is our new little darling.
He licks my head while I am relaxing.
He wakes Jane up when it is time to go to bed.
And when he does not get his own way
He does not tolerate it and uses his head.
By ripping up the carpet and meowing
And playing with the buttons on the settee
He will get you to clean his poo pit.
Or give him a snack eventually.
He is thoughtful and very entertaining.
And we appreciate and love him.